Seabird
in the
Forest

The Mystery of the Marbled Murrelet

Joan Dunning

Boyds Mills Press

Honesdale, Pennsylvania

Acknowledgments

With gratitude and deep appreciation, I extend my thanks to the following scientists and experts
who offered their knowledge and guidance in the writing and illustrating of this book:

Thomas B. Dunklin, photographer and videographer

David Fix, senior author of *Birds of Northern California* (Lone Pine Publishing, 2000)

Richard T. Golightly, professor, Department of Wildlife, Humboldt State University, Arcata, California

Ron LeValley, founder and senior biologist, Mad River Biologists, Eureka, California

Sherri Miller, wildlife biologist, Redwood Sciences Laboratory,
Pacific Southwest Research Station, Arcata, California

S. Kim Nelson, senior faculty research assistant, Department of Fisheries and Wildlife,
Oregon State University, Corvallis, Oregon

Charles Powell, past litigation coordinator, Environmental Protection Information Center (EPIC), Redway, California

C. John Ralph, research wildlife biologist and technical editor of *Ecology and Conservation of the Marbled Murrelet*
(U.S. Department of Agriculture, Forest Service, Pacific Southwest Research Station, 1995, 2010)

Maria Mudd Ruth, author of *Rare Bird: Pursuing the Mystery of the Marbled Murrelet* (Rodale, 2005)

Stephen C. Sillett, professor and Kenneth L. Fisher Chair in Redwood Forest Ecology, Department of Forestry
and Wildland Resources, Humboldt State University, Arcata, California

A profound thank you to my editor, Karen Klockner. Even though she lives thousands of miles
from the forests of the Pacific Northwest, she has always believed in this book.

Boyds Mills Press, Inc.
815 Church Street
Honesdale, Pennsylvania 18431
CIP data is available.

First edition
Book design by Amy Drinker, Aster Designs
The text of this book is set in 14-point Janson and 10.5-point ITC Flora.
10 9 8 7 6 5 4 3 2 1

Alaska

CANADA

PACIFIC OCEAN

Washington

Oregon

California

Nevada

Author's Note

In 1974, a strange, downy chick was found, sitting all alone, high in a tree in Big Basin Redwoods State Park, south of San Francisco, California. This little bird was the answer to a nearly two-hundred-year-old mystery— the mystery of the marbled murrelet. The location of the nesting place of the marbled murrelet was the last of any bird in all of North America to be discovered, because few people could imagine that a tiny seabird with webbed feet might nest miles inland, high in the canopy of the tallest and some of the most ancient trees on earth. This book is the story of one such chick.

Out on the wide Pacific Ocean,

the light of dawn is just filtering through the fog, revealing two

small brown-and-white seabirds. They are so at home on the

ocean swells, it is as if they are playing—bobbing on the surface

and then suddenly diving to pursue tiny, glinting silver fish.

For most of the year, through giant Pacific storms and calm

Pacific days, the ocean is their home, always rocking, always

rolling, with the waves that come from far away. Beneath the

birds, fronds of giant kelp reach upward from the dark depths.

It seems as if the birds could float and dive and doze forever

among the leafy treetops of this towering underwater forest.

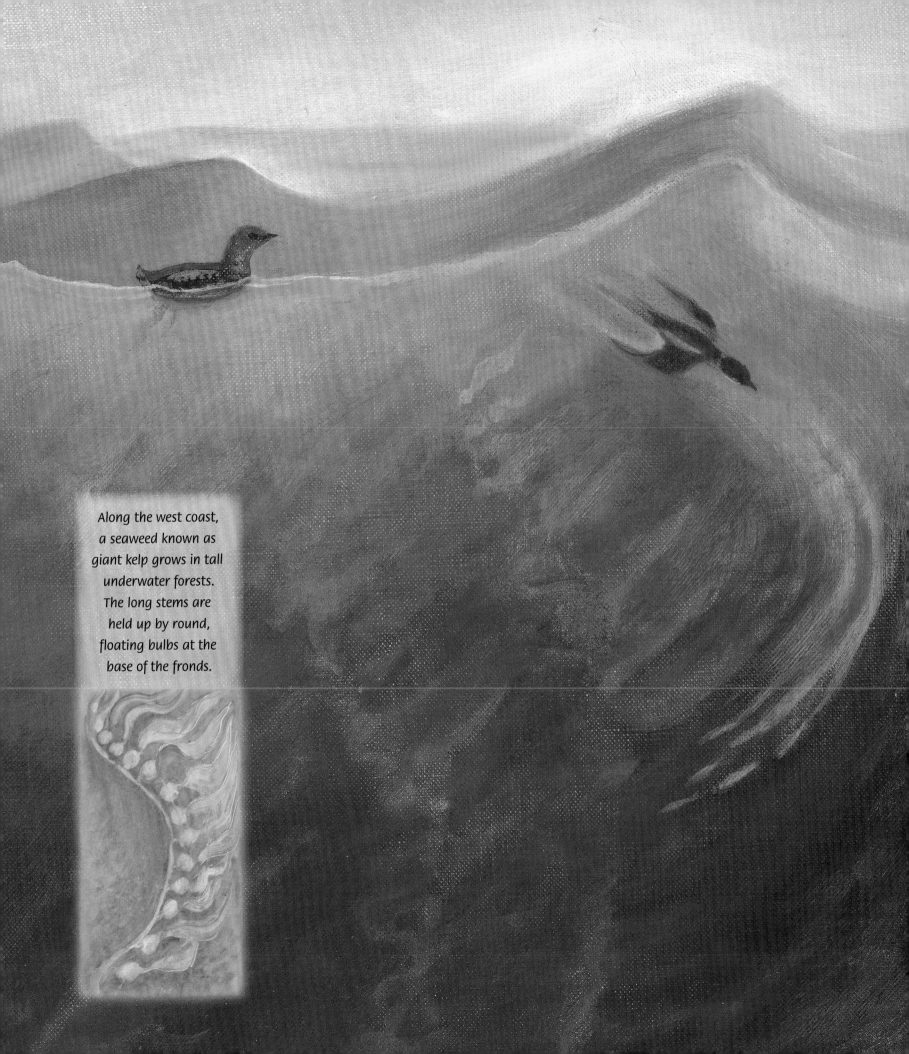

Along the west coast, a seaweed known as giant kelp grows in tall underwater forests. The long stems are held up by round, floating bulbs at the base of the fronds.

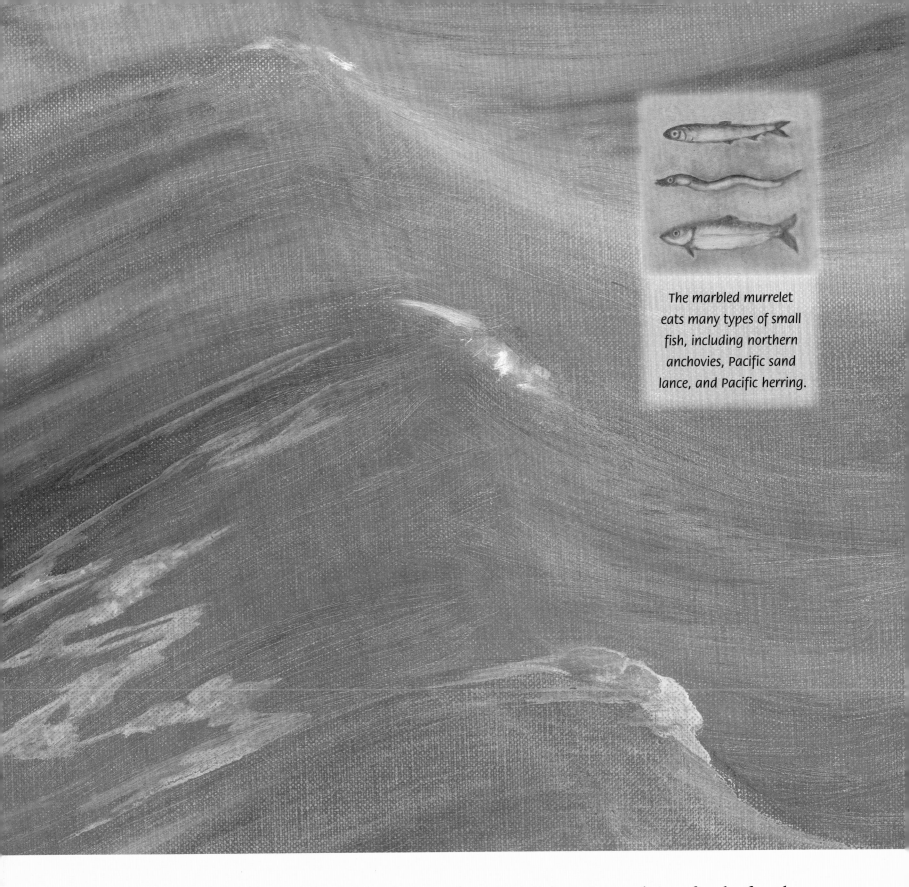

The marbled murrelet eats many types of small fish, including northern anchovies, Pacific sand lance, and Pacific herring.

But there is a different forest that beckons to them now. It is spring and time for the female seabird to lay her one, single egg. She cannot lay it on the rolling surface of the ocean or attach it to a leafy frond of kelp or drop it into the water the way fish do. She is a bird, and her egg must be kept warm and dry, not just for one or two days, but for a whole month.

The marbled murrelet uses its wings to "fly" while diving underwater. But it is also very good at flying through the air. It can fly at speeds over sixty miles per hour.

Most seabirds simply fly to the safety of offshore rocks and islands and lay their eggs on bare ground or in burrows. But not these birds. They are marbled murrelets. For nearly two hundred years, people tried to figure out where the marbled murrelet hatches and raises its young, but not one nest could be found. For the murrelets, however, the location of their nests has never been a mystery. It is early morning, before dawn, and the two birds are awake and ready. They flap their wings, and their bodies lift clear of the water.

"Marbled" refers to the feathers on the marbled murrelet's breast, which have a swirly pattern like marble. "Murrelet" comes from the word "murre," which is the name of a larger seabird relative of the murrelet. Adding "let" to the end of a word makes it refer to something smaller in size—a "droplet" is a little drop, and a "piglet" is a little pig. The murrelet is one of the smallest relatives of the murre.

"Keer, keer!" With soft, gull-like cries, the murrelets call to one another. "Keer! Keer! Keer!" The little seabirds fly swiftly away from the safety of the ocean.

Though the coast redwood is the tallest tree on earth, its cone is very small, only about as big as an olive. Young redwoods also sprout from the roots of older trees, known as "grandmother trees." When these giant grandmothers finally fall, the younger trees are still left standing in what is called a "fairy ring."

A camper, just waking and stepping from a tent, might look up and notice two tiny birds flying by. He or she might hear the faint "Keer! Keer! Keer!" but that person would probably have no idea where the birds came from or where they are going. They would look like two brown dots with wings, now here, now gone.

Because the nesting place of the marbled murrelet was discovered so recently, and because the forest canopy is such a secret place, biologists still have much to learn about these birds. With a camera that must be put in place before the breeding season begins, scientists have observed one pair of murrelets using the same nest tree for nine years. From such observations, it is believed that marbled murrelets pair for life or until one of the pair dies. Then the other bird will find a new mate. If the nest tree is cut down, the birds may stop nesting altogether. Biologists are not sure where marbled murrelets mate—on the ocean or on the nest branch.

But the birds know where they are going. In the dark forest they seek one particular tree where they have laid their egg in years past. They slow their flight, using their webbed feet as brakes in the air, and land on a large limb. Here it is strangely still after life on the rolling ocean, and stillness is what they need. The female shuffles down the limb toward the trunk and settles her body into the shadows.

Although a murrelet is only as big as a robin, it lays an egg that is nearly as big as a chicken's. This allows the murrelet's one chick to be quite large, fully downed, and able to be left alone within days. A robin, by comparison, usually lays three to five much smaller eggs, and its chicks are tiny, naked, and helpless when hatched.

Even though the egg is still inside her, it already contains a new life. She feels the egg gradually move down through her body and out onto the limb. She stands with a new lightness and then settles once more. Now there is only one job: to keep the egg safe and warm. The female's marbled feathers camouflage her, providing the egg's only protection.

The Steller's Jay is native to western North America. Even though it is approximately the same size as a marbled murrelet, it is a frequent predator of the murrelet chicks as well as other species of baby birds. It also feeds on human food and garbage.

If a jay or a raven catches sight of her, she may be pushed off the nest and the egg pecked open and eaten. So she must sit as still as possible, rising only occasionally to turn the egg, then settling to absolute stillness. Meanwhile, the male drops off the limb, and his rapidly beating wings carry him back to the sea to fish, so he can be ready to take his turn incubating the egg.

Many shrubs and even trees grow in the soil that collects on the limbs of ancient trees. Huckleberry bushes, salal, tan oak, spruce, hemlock, pepperwood, and Douglas-fir are at home growing hundreds of feet above the ground on the limb of a giant tree.

The canopy of upper branches of the ancient trees has a life of its own, remote from the ground far below. In the hollows and crevices of the bark, fallen twigs and needles collect, decomposing over centuries into rich soil. Ferns root in the soil, developing into large, thick mats that store water from fog and rain, releasing it slowly in trickling "canopy waterfalls." Through this soil wander earthworms that never touch the ground during their entire lives. Shrubs take root in the soil, their flowers pollinated by wild bees, producing edible berries. Even trees sprout in the soil, growing many feet tall. No wonder a bird from a family of ground-nesters feels at home here. It is a landscape above a landscape.

The next dawn, the male suddenly returns. Now it is his turn to warm the egg. The parents exchange places, and the father settles down while the female slips away. The male dozes with the egg safe beneath him. The forest is so different from the ocean, the whole canopy barely swaying with the breeze. The song of a varied thrush filters up from below in long, single, mysterious notes that seem to make time stand still. For a whole month the two birds take turns—one on the nest while the other is fishing or sleeping on the rolling surface of the ocean.

Marbled murrelets generally nest within twenty miles of the ocean, but they have been known to travel as far as fifty miles inland to find a suitable nest tree. This means that an adult might fly a hundred miles, round trip, to deliver just one small fish to its chick.

That evening, the father lands on the limb with a little silver fish in his beak! It looks too big for the chick to swallow, but the chick begins begging, bobbing his body up and down, up and down, exercising new muscles. Suddenly, the chick has it in his own beak. He holds it tightly, pausing as if surprised. The fish is rich and salty and tastes like the ocean far, far away. As if he has done this many times before, the chick suddenly turns the fish to point headfirst down his throat and swallows it in two deep gulps.

The wandering salamander is at home high in the canopy, eating earthworms and small insects that live there. The salamander needs to remain wet, so it waits for rainy or foggy days to travel along the branches and even straight up or down the trunk of the tree. The female salamander lays her eggs in damp crevices and hollows, and guards them until they hatch. A wandering salamander might never touch the ground for its entire life.

The chick's parents take turns brooding him, keeping him warm until his body is able to warm itself. Then, one morning, his mother suddenly drops from the limb, leaving the chick all alone. There is no tiny fence to keep him from falling off. Only instinct keeps him safe. For thousands of years murrelet chicks have simply waited, all alone, high above the forest floor, waited for their parents to return each day with little silver fish … waited a whole month to grow up … and so will this one.

Day follows night. Night follows day. The chick's parents come and go, bringing him fish. Fog rolls in for days at a time, erasing the chick's world with its mysterious whiteness and hiding him from the ravens and jays that swoop through the canopy. The chick pecks at the fog-dampened moss and receives a tiny drink. Though the fog soaks the outer layer of his thick down, inside he is still warm and dry, and when the fog burns off and the days are hot and sunny, his down serves as insulation to keep him cool. As long as he remains unseen—one whole month as a living secret—nature provides for all his needs.

Northern flying squirrels live in the canopy, raising their young in the secret cavities in the trunk and teaching them to glide from tree to tree. They sail on the capes of skin that stretch between their front and back legs.

A sliver of moon hangs in the night sky. A spotted owl hoots. A northern flying squirrel is teaching her young to glide. Bats have emerged from hollows in the trees and are hunting insects, swooping and darting. It seems as if everyone gets to fly except one little, fluffy marbled murrelet chick.

A hoary bat has chosen a small branch nearby. Each morning, after a night of chasing moths through the shadowy canopy, she folds her wings and hangs upside down to sleep.

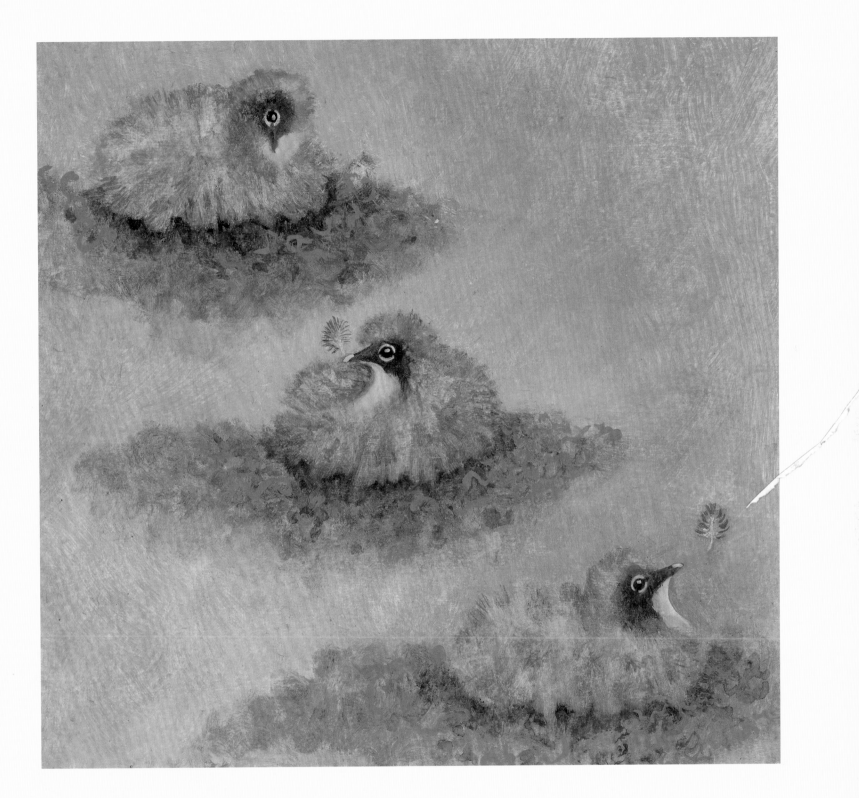

Then one morning the chick begins doing a curious thing. He reaches back and plucks off one of his own fine, downy feathers and sends it sailing on the breeze. He pauses and then reaches back again and plucks another … and another, sending them drifting through the air. He does this all day and into the night until, when the light of the next dawn shines down on the nest …

Seen from above, a small bird with a dark back will blend in with the surface of the ocean, protecting it from predatory gulls. The bird's white underside will blend with the brightness of the sky, making it difficult to see from below.

he has turned into a black-and-white seabird! While he has spent a month on the limb getting bigger and stronger, black-and-white feathers have also been growing beneath his downy camouflage. Now, just a little bit of his down remains on the back of his head—where he can't reach with his beak. Suddenly, he is a seabird out of place in the forest. It is time to leave.

Sometimes a murrelet parent returns to the nest after the chick has flown. The adult holds a fish in its beak and waits. Finally, it may fly off, still holding the fish.

The chick stands, stretches his wings again, flaps them, and shuffles to the edge of the branch. He pauses, and then, after a month of sitting still, he simply jumps into thin air to rely on wings he has never tried before. He flaps hard as he begins to fall, and the air supports him. He straightens out and flies, weaving at great speed among the giant trees of the forest, the only home he has ever known. Then he spots the faint glistening of a creek far, far below.

In the state and national parks, the forests are protected from logging. But clearcuts often come right up to the boundaries of the parks, providing sharp contrast. When as little as forty percent of the trees are left standing, soil is held in place by their roots and the whole ecosystem, including rivers and streams, benefits.

He follows the sparkling creek. It flows into a larger river, and he follows that. He crosses the boundary of the state park where he was hatched, and suddenly below him, the trees are gone. The land is harsh and exposed, with bulldozed dirt roads winding across bare earth. But he keeps flying, and suddenly the trees are below him again, soft and inviting once more.

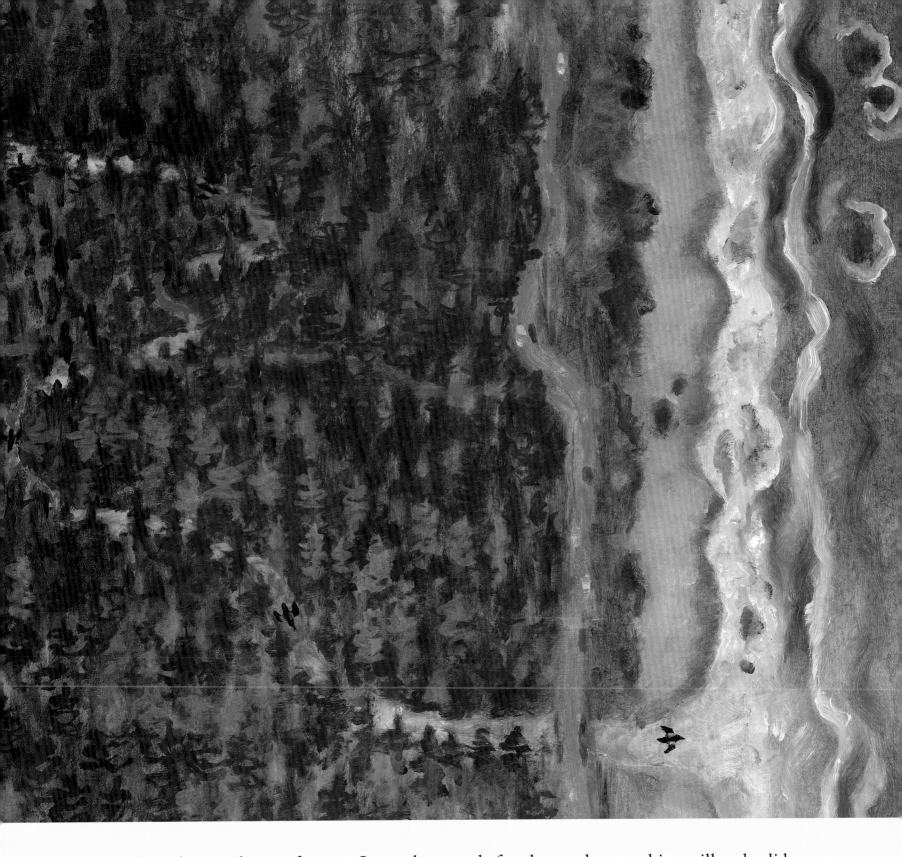

But he is done with trees for now. It may be years before he touches anything still and solid again. He crosses a road with little dots of cars speeding north and south and then swoops over a swath of gray sand. Now there is nothing but the white, rolling waves coming forward to greet him, rumbling and tumbling with water … water … and more water. Then there is blue—the blue of open water dotted with other murrelets at home on the sea.

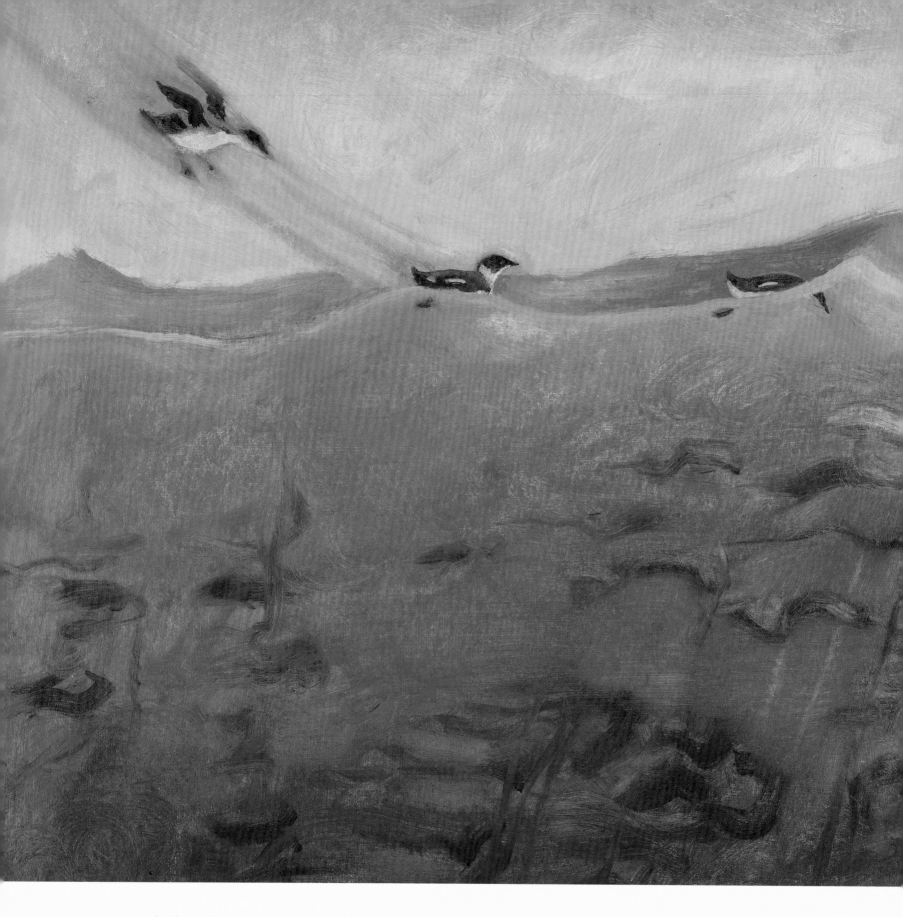

He splashes down, and the cold water holds him with ease. He paddles his webbed feet and is propelled speedily across the surface. He drops his head underwater, and a whole new world opens up beneath him.

He flips into a dive, spreading his wings as if he is flying, veering this way and that as if he had been swimming all his life, and then … what does he see?

A little silver fish!

Sources

Books

A Field Guide to Nests, Eggs, and Nestlings of North American Birds by Colin Harrison (Collins, 1978)

Birds of Northern California by David Fix (Lone Pine Publishing, 2000)

Ecology and Conservation of the Marbled Murrelet, C. John Ralph, George L. Hunt, Martin G. Raphael, and John F. Piatt, Technical Editors (U.S. Department of Agriculture, Forest Service, Pacific Southwest Research Station, 1995, 2010)

Forest Giants of the Pacific Coast by Robert Van Pelt (Global Forest Society/University of Washington Press, 2001)

The Marbled Murrelets of the Caren Range and Middlepoint Bight by Paul Harris Jones
(Western Canada Wilderness Committee, Canada, 2001)

Rare Bird: Pursuing the Mystery of the Marbled Murrelet by Maria Mudd Ruth (Rodale, 2005)

Secrets of the Old Growth Forest by David Kelly; photographs by Gary Braasch (Gibbs-Smith, 1988)

Web Sites

Centre for Wildlife Ecology, Simon Fraser University: www.sfu.ca/biology/wildberg/

Institute for Redwood Ecology, Humboldt State University: www.humboldt.edu/redwoods

Environmental Protection Information Center (EPIC), Redway, California: www.wildcalifornia.org

Maria Ruth: www.mariaruthbooks.com

National Park Service, U.S. Department of the Interior:
www.nps.gov/redw/naturescience/marbled-murrelet.htm

Thomas B. Dunklin's Web site: www.thomasbdunklin.com/gallery/RedwoodForests

U.S. Fish and Wildlife Service: www.fws.gov/desfbay/Archives/Murrelet/murrelet.htm

Western Canada Wilderness Committee: www.wildernesscommittee.mb.ca

Coast redwoods have adapted to withstand fire, and healthy trees often have burned-out hollows at various places on their trunks. Hollows that are low to the ground are called goose-pen trees, because settlers used them as houses for their livestock. Whether at ground level or high up in the canopy, these charred hollows also make valuable homes for many wild animals.

A trunk can span 25 feet in diameter.

A 6-foot tall person

Biologists who study the giant trees use a powerful bow to shoot an arrow carrying a line over one of the lowest branches. Then they attach a rope to the line, and haul it up. They climb with the utmost care, generally suspending themselves in midair, touching the trees as little as possible to avoid damaging delicate lichens, moss, and other life forms. They are not allowed to climb during the murrelet breeding season.